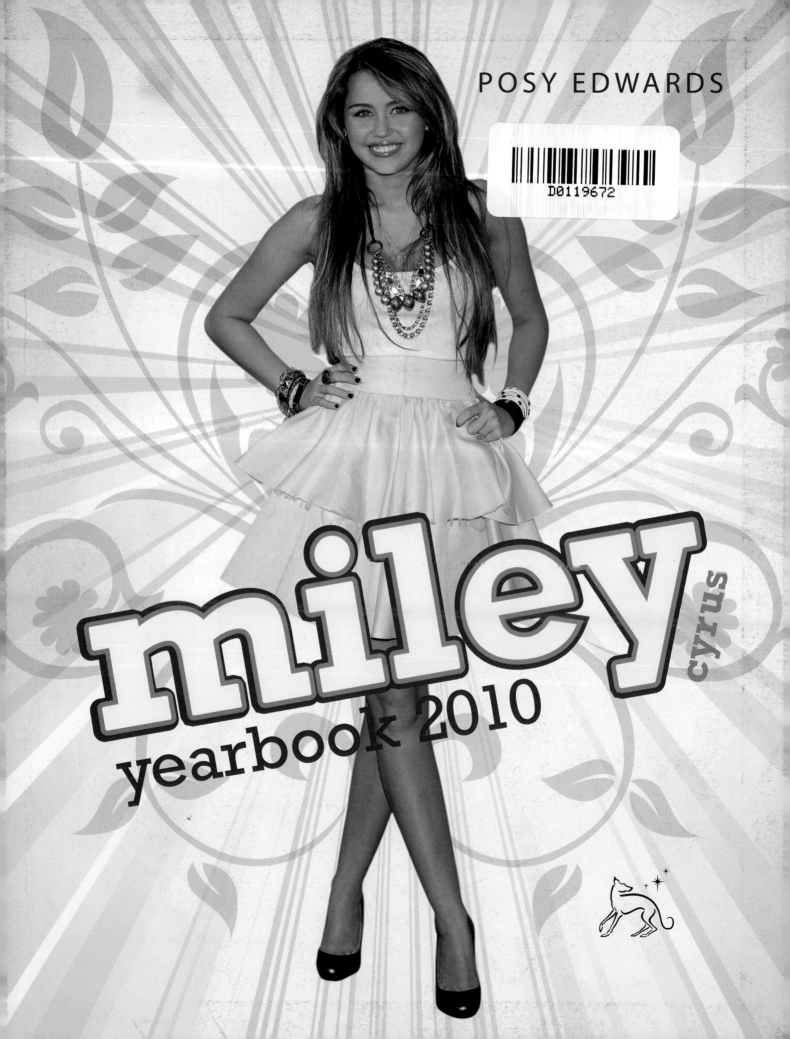

POSY EDWARDS

miley cyrus
yearbook 2010

From Smiley to Miley

EARLY DAYS AND FAMILY LIFE

For Billy Ray Cyrus, 1992 wasn't a year he was going to forget in a hurry. For starters, "Achy Breaky Heart", the song that made him an instant legend in country music, shot to number one in the charts. Just to top it all off though, November 23rd 1992 was the date that a young girl who was given the name of Destiny Hope Cyrus was born. The moment her proud, perfect-haired father looked into her dazzling eyes and saw her give him the sort of smile that would lead to her being called Smiley, he knew that he had a future star on his hands.

Just like the zany Stewarts in *Hannah Montana*, the Cyrus family would travel together on the road as Billy Ray toured the world with his chart-topping country tunes. Little Destiny was having such a fun and happy time touring with her father that she never stopped smiling, even as a teething toddler. Her ever-present flashing smile soon earned her the nickname "Smiley". After some years this was shortened to "Miley", the name she's used ever since. In 2008, Miley made it official and legally changed her name from Destiny to Miley, using Ray as her new middle name as a testament to her dad – how sweet! Only her grandma still sticks with tradition and insists on calling her granddaughter by her christened name, Destiny.

Just like Miley's crazy gang of friends and family in *Hannah Montana*, the teen star has been surrounded by her whacky friends and family since day one. And she's always grateful for the loving environment she was brought up in.

"Some people don't have a family to fall back on, like I have. That's what keeps me strong," says Miley.

Her home was always a madhouse, as along with Miley there is her half-brother Christopher Cody, Billy Ray's adopted stepchildren Trace and Brandi, Miley's younger brother Braison and her younger sister, Noah. Miley and Braison are not that unlike Hannah and Jackson. They always care and look out for each other, but love nothing more than winding one another up. Braison once put a wooden snake in Miley's bed – you should have heard her squeal!

Before moving to LA, Miley and her clan of siblings lived on a ranch in Nashville, Tennessee. When she wasn't on the road touring with her rock star dad, she had the most wondrous childhood playing with horses, dogs, cats and chicks. Before she could hardly walk, she was galloping around the ranch on horseback, living out a typical cowgirl fantasy. Now she's a worldwide TV and pop star, Miley has fewer opportunities to make it back to her southern US roots, and it's things like mucking out the stables and braiding her horses' tails that she misses most about home. One day, when all of this Hollywood mania is over, she'd love nothing more than to set up a big old ranch, just like the one she grew up on, and having herself weekly hoedowns and the like. Yee haw, cowgirl!

A YOUNG STAR . . .

With a rockin' and rolling father like Billy Ray, not to mention having Dolly Parton – the queen of country and western – as her godmother, it was inevitable that Miley would be singing as soon as she was able to crawl. "My dad says I could sing before I could talk, if that's possible. I was always humming and things like that," says Miley. At the teeny age of only two years old, she was already warming up for her role of playing superstar Hannah Montana as she would waddle on stage to sing with her dad: "I would sing 'Hound Dog' and silly songs for the fun of it."

Her superstar qualities were there for all to see from a very young age. She was forever parading around the house in front of people and she revelled in attention:

"When I was little, I would stand up on couches and exclaim, Watch me! We had these showers that are completely glass, and I would lock people in them and make them stay in there and watch me perform."

Wow, imagine watching a private performance from Hannah Montana? You should be so lucky!

So from day one Miley was following her destiny to sing and dance through life. But she didn't always receive applause for her performances. Remember the *Hannah Montana* episode where Miley was forced to be a pirate, her school's mascot, instead of a cheerleader? Well, she knows all about embarrassing herself in front of her school pals. When trying out for her school dance team, she fell over and ripped her denim skirt in front of all the boys while practising in the school hallway. Needless to say, her face was as red as a ripe tomato with embarrassment!

AUDITION LIMBO

In 2005, the execs at Disney were considering the idea of making a show based on a *That's So Raven* episode in which a child star of a popular TV show attends a local school and tries to lead a normal life. Initially, they couldn't decide on a name and Anna Cabana, Samantha York and Alexis Texas were all possibilities. With the name of the show still not confirmed, auditions began under the working title *The Secret Life of Zoe Stewart*.

Initially, Miley tried out for the role of best friend Lilly, but the execs just loved her husky singing voice and felt she should try out for the starring role. Never one to shy away from a greater challenge, Miley was delighted to take on the task of landing the lead role.

However, a thousand other young starlets were in with a shot, so Miley had just an outside chance of getting the part. She was only 11 years old and the role required her to portray a 14 year old. Her competitors were far taller, not to mention more experienced.

This all made the audition process terrifying for Miley, who admits to feeling very intimidated: "You walk into a room with sixty girls … You can see their head-shots and just know they know a lot more than you do. In my case, I have to say, if I was them I don't know why they chose me." Standing in front of a bunch of people and having every part of your appearance judged and scrutinised must be pretty terrifying stuff! As Miley explains:

"They don't like you – that is the scariest part! I did taping. I did two tapes, four tapes. I started out as Lilly and they wanted me to audition for the main role and that sounded very positive. But they said, 'You are too small, too young. Bye-bye.' Well, that's rude. So I made another tape. Dang it! They are going to watch my tape and like it!"

Despite being too short and too young, the casting directors did like the tape and she was allowed to stay in the running for the lead part.

But still Miley wasn't even close to nailing her dream role. She had to go through audition after audition in full knowledge that her dreams could crumble at any time if she were to be sent home. Just like her TV character, though, Miley's a feisty battler who never gives up, no matter what.

"I auditioned forever. At first they said I was too small and too young. But afterwards I was like, 'One more time? I can dress up differently! I can look older!' So I kept trying out and it was still no, so I freaked out!"

Despite the continued rejection, Miley still persisted. Even when it seemed that everything was against her, and disaster struck on one of her final auditions, she still stuck at it. "I had lost my teeth before the audition, my front teeth; four of them had braces on top. Even though I talk a lot, my mouth and face is tiny. I was sitting there with huge buckteeth and huge braces and huge hair and a tiny little body. But four months later the producers were like, Come to California." So braces and all, when it came

The Hannah & Miley QUIZ

Think you know everything there is to know about the honkey tonk heroine and the rockin' and rollin' rock superstar? Take the Hannah quiz and see how many points you can score to find out if you're her biggest know-it-all fan.

1 Which one of these is a nickname Hannah has sometimes been called on the show?
- a) Hannah Montaney
- b) H-Dog
- c) H-to-the-M
- d) Hannah-Smiley-Miley

2 Which of these is one of Hannah and Miley's favourite phrases when she's frustrated?
- a) Holy Moly!
- b) Friggin' Hell!
- c) Oh Sugar!
- d) Sweet Niblets!

3 What is the name of Miley's favourite cuddly toy?
- a) Cuddles
- b) Kitty
- c) Pooh
- d) Beary

4 In one episode of Hannah Montana, Miley has a dream about Lilly having a crush on someone, who was this?
- a) Rico
- b) Jake
- c) Jackson
- d) Mr Corelli

5 What is the name of the school Miley attends?
- a) Fairview
- b) Seaview
- c) Niceview
- d) Oceanview

6 Miley and Hannah both have the help of their two best friends, but what are their full names?
- a) Lilly Truscott and Oliver Oken
- b) Lilly Treehugger and Oliver Oakhead
- c) Lilly Turnip and Oliver Oblong
- d) Lilly Truckdriver and Oliver Owleyes

7 When Hannah appeared on a cooking show, she told everyone what food she hated the most, which food was this?
- a) Onions
- b) Broccoli
- c) Carrots
- d) Cauliflower

8 During one episode, Miley's mean brother Jackson suddenly starts behaving nice to her, what caused this?
- a) Being hypnotised
- b) Losing his memory
- c) Eating too much chocolate
- d) Watching too much TV

9 In Hannah Montana: The Movie, what is the name of the sneaky reporter who knows Miley's secret?
- a) Oswald
- b) Oscar
- c) Sherlock
- d) George

10 Before the show had even started and Miley Cyrus was a star, which part did she try out for?
- a) Amber
- b) Lilly
- c) Aunt Dolly
- d) Jackson

11 Which of these places is Miley scared of?
- a) Dentist's
- b) Vet's
- c) Hospital
- d) All of them

12 Which one of these was Miley's crush at one point?
- a) Johnny Collins
- b) Donny
- c) Cooper
- d) Colin Lasseter

13 What special trick does Miley try to use sometimes to get her own way when she's asking her dad for something?
- a) Gets down on her knees
- b) Does puppy dog eyes
- c) Makes her lips tremble
- d) Makes him breakfast

14 Hannah performs loads of songs in her show, but which song does she perform in her pyjamas?
- a) "Make Some Noise"
- b) "True Friend"
- c) "Pumpin' Up the Party"
- d) "This is the Life"

15 When Hannah goes away for a while to star in a film, who does she find have started dating when she returns?
- a) Tina and Joey Vitolo
- b) Derek and Sarah
- c) Mikayla and Donny
- d) Lilly and Ollie

16 When Miley goes out on a date with a cute guy named Connor, she is put off when she finds out something about him, what?
- a) Bad breath
- b) Awful fashion sense
- c) Too short
- d) Squeaky voice

17 What are the names of the people who dislike Miley the most at Seaview?
- a) Josie and Molly
- b) Jane and Amanda
- c) Lisa and Linda
- d) Amber and Ashley

18 In Hannah Montana: The Movie Miley misses the birthday of someone close to her, which friend was this?
- a) Lilly
- b) Rico
- c) Ollie
- d) Jackson

19 What is the name of the drink Robby likes to make that can sometimes have weird side effects?
- a) Toffee-Flavoured Coffee
- b) Loco Hot Cocoa
- c) Pea Sweet Tea
- d) Ready-Made Fizzy Lemonade

20 Even though Hannah Montana is one of the coolest names on the planet, what did the makers of the show want to call it at first?
- a) *Double Life*
- b) *Better Days*
- c) *Rock n' Roll Princess*
- d) *Best of Both Worlds*

How many did you score? Add up your points to see just how much of a brain box on Hannah and Miley you really are. The answers can be found on page 61.

16–20 You know more about Hannah and Miley than Miss Cyrus herself! You are her number one fan!

11–15 Wow! You really do know your stuff! Miley is lucky to have you as a fan!

6–10 You know your facts, just not enough of them. You're a half-hearted Hannah fan.

0–5 You need to brush up on your knowledge. You're a mediocre Miley fan.

Miley's Favourite Episodes in Season Two

Episodes 9 and 10: Achy Jakey Heart

A double-bill episode, in which Jake Ryan returns. Miley quickly gives in to Jake's charms and ends up telling him her secret, and then finding out how difficult the heartthrob finds life without getting constantly treated like a star. Eventually, Miley is left with no choice but to dump the cutie pie superstar.

Episode 12: When You Wish You were the Star

In this memorable episode, Miley wishes she could be Hannah Montana all the time, but finds out it isn't all it's cracked up to be. Despite being able to date celeb Jesse McCartney – hubba hubba! – Miley is quick to realise that being a worldwide celebrity all the time isn't the best way to live your life.

Episode 18: That's What Friends are For

Jake Ryan returns once more. He assures Miley that he won't spill her secret to anyone, and asks Miley if they could just be friends. Miley was unsure at first, and becomes even more so when she finds out Jake is cast alongside Hannah's arch-enemy, Mikayla!

Episode 16: Me and Mr Jonas and Mr Jonas and Mr Jonas

It's pretty obvious why Miley loves this episode so much, as her supercrush Nick Jonas stars in it! Though Miley is initially jealous that it's her dad rather than her who gets to spend all the time with the Jonas brothers writing songs, Hannah Montana eventually is lucky enough to join in with them!

Episode 26: Yet Another Side of Me

Miley decides it's time for a change in Hannah's image after she is influenced by her idol, the musician Isis, who constantly changes image to keep her constant attention and music fresh. Hannah becomes scared of losing her audience if she doesn't follow Isis' example, but the new look doesn't become popular and she learns that it's more important to stick to what you know and not allow yourself to be influenced so easily.

HANNAH MONTANA: SEASON TWO

With Miley starting high school, and having more responsibilities in her life, she learns to balance school and showbiz much better than she ever has before. A major event in Season Two is the return of Jake Ryan, Miley's love interest in Season One.

Once again, Miley is faced with the problem of whether she reveals her secret identity to another person. Will she need to do it for anyone to get close to her? Or is she so good at hiding it now that it doesn't matter whether they know or not?

As if Miley didn't have enough enemies in high school, Hannah now finds an enemy in the annoying Mikayla, a pop star who pretends to be Hannah's friend in public, but secretly hates her in real life!

HANNAH MONTANA: SEASON THREE

Now that Miley is older and more mature, she has finally found a much better balance between her and Hannah's lives. Season Three is about how the characters begin to grow up and try to get more responsibility in their lives, though they find out that sometimes they don't want it just yet.

Important changes start to happen in Miley's life, such as trying to get her driver's licence, which leads to some major embarrassment at a party! And getting her own bank account to let her spend her own money – just think of how many shoes she could buy!

As Miley gets older, she also gets smarter! In Season Three she is now working out how to use her fame much better. Whether it's getting her driver's licence or pretending to date a fellow star for extra fame, it's clear that Miley is now smarter, sharper and more grown up than we've ever seen her before!

Miley's Favourite Episodes in Season Three

Episode 2: Ready, Set, Don't Drive

Miley is finally ready to show off her awesome driving skills so she can get her licence, and that will mean fulfilling every girl's dream and having no more embarrassing lifts from her dad! Unfortunately it doesn't exactly go according to plan as her driving instructor is so disgusting that she can't help but throw him out in the middle of her exam. Miley then goes as Hannah to get her licence, knowing that nobody would be able to say no to one of the most famous girls on the planet! But as she's driving to a party and gets pulled over for speeding she suddenly realises that she got her licence as Hannah Montana rather than Miley! After a gruelling test from a Hannah fan to convince everyone that she is the rock princess they all know and love, Miley's worst nightmare comes back as her dad ends up driving her to the party! Hannah did however learn the important lesson that no matter how much you want something you should never bend the rules, because as her dad says it will only bite you in the butt!

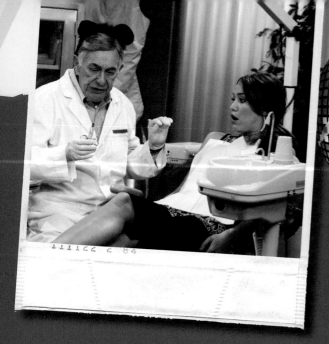

Episode 4: You Never Give Me my Money

When Miley asks for a raise in her allowance, just imagine how she feels when her dad not only lets her open her own bank account but also gives her $5000! Miley, however, tries to exercise self-control and buys nothing, giving her cheque book away to make sure that she doesn't, after the crazy credit card spending you might remember in Season One! Meanwhile, even though Robby knows where Jackson's missing phone is, he decides to have some fun and let Jackson go absolutely insane while he tries to find it!

Episode 5: Killing Me Softly with his Height

While shopping at the mall, Miley is introduced to Connor. Connor seems to have everything; he is super-cute and makes her laugh so she agrees to go on a date with him. Unfortunately Miley is put off when she realises that he is so short he can't even reach up to kiss her! Things don't go well when Miley points out how short he is, and Connor ends the date feeling very hurt. Miley becomes determined to have a second chance with him, learning not to judge a guy on something as meaningless as his height and that a great personality is what really matters.

Episode 8: Welcome to the Bungle

Disaster strikes as, while Hannah Montana is on a cookery show, she reveals that she can't stand carrots. Because of what she says, her loyal fans decide to follow her example and stop eating carrots! Unfortunately, when she goes back on the show to explain herself, she ends up accidentally saying that she hates reading! Eventually Miley resolves the problem by telling the truth, learning about how responsible she needs to be with her fame when setting an example.

Episode 10: Cheat It

To help her record sales, Hannah pretends to be dating the ultra-gorgeous singer Austin Rain. Unfortunately, when Miley finds out Jackson is planning on cheating in his history test, she tells him that cheating is wrong and dishonest – but she is being dishonest by having a fake boyfriend. Miley eventually realises that she would have to come clean to convince Jackson, who had learnt all the answers while he was pretending to cheat anyway! Both of them realise that being dishonest will never make people think any better of you, only worse.

Miley CROSSWORD

Are you a Miley superfan? Test yourself on the questions below and see if they fit into the grid!

ACROSS

6 Miley's nickname as a child

7 The first name used for *Hannah Montana* when the show was still a work in progress

9 The episode of *Hannah Montana* in which Hannah pretends to date singer Austin Rain

11 Miley's first Disney cover

12 Miley's younger brother

DOWN

1 Miley's current boyfriend

2 Miley's age when she auditioned for *Hannah Montana*

3 Miley's real life BFF

4 The name of Miley's first single

5 Miley's first album

8 The name of Miley's Yorkshire Terrier

10 Miley's other first name

Make-Up

Miley always needs to look her best. Whether it's performing in concert or just popping down to the store to buy some cookie dough (mmmmmmm, Miley's favourite!) it's hard work looking fabulous for those cameras all the time. She always manages to pull it off though!

Here are some of Miley's best tips so you can be ready for that next party and look great, just like her!

Miley's Make-Up Tip

Vaseline is a must-have! Smother it on your eyelashes at night and wake up with soft, silky lashes. Slick over your lips for a glossy sheen and a superstar-perfect pout! Or even smooth it over your eye shadow for lasting hold and to brighten up those beautiful eyes!

THE MILEY LOOK

When it comes to make-up, Miley has always said she prefers the natural look: plenty of lip gloss and some nice girly pink tones. She also likes to use black mascara, eye shadow, plenty of pink blusher, and a tiny amount of concealer if she has any blemishes. Use a mirror to copy the shape of your hair and eyebrows on to the face below, and design your own make-up look. Why not use a crayon or a felt-tip to try out different colours on the eyelids, cheeks and lips to find that perfect, rock-star look for you?

Essentials for your make-up bag:

Blusher – peach or pink

Lip Gloss – pink or red

Shimmer Dust – for your cheeks

Eye Shadow – the colour depends on who you want to be. Miley uses light pinks, golds, creams and natural browns. Hannah, on the other hand, wears greens, yellows and purples.

Black Eyeliner – either liquid or kohl pencil. It's a good idea to check with your mum!

Mascara – brown or black

Make-up brushes

GIVE YOURSELF A MILEY MANICURE

1 In order to achieve a cute yet glam manicure like Miley, your nails must be clean and neat. Fill a bowl with warm water and add a couple of drops of lavender oil, or even bath salts or bubbles. Soak hands in water for five minutes to soften skin and wash away any dirt.

2 If your nails are too long – Miley prefers to keep hers short and sweet – give them a trim with a pair of nail scissors. Then, using a nail file, smooth down the tips of your nails, making sure that every fingernail is the same length and shape.

3 Now for the fun part… pick a colour! Miley always matches the colour of her nails with her mood and outfit: she loves bright, girly hot pinks for concerts or on the red carpet; grungy black nails suit her dressed-down, rock-star style; and pale, neutral colours, such as light pinks or a clear glaze, give Miley a casual, natural daytime look.

4 Give the nail varnish bottle a good shake before opening it. With a steady hand, coat each nail evenly, gliding upwards with the brush from the base to the tip. If you make a mistake, don't panic! Simply use a cotton bud dipped in nail polish remover to clean up any mess.

5 Wait about ten minutes for nails to dry. Use a second coat of varnish so that the nail paint doesn't chip, and remains bold and glossy for longer. If you are feeling especially stylish, glitz up your nails with gems and stickers: hearts and stars are Miley's personal favs! A thin coat of clear varnish can be painted over stickers to give them extra hold.

Your fabulous fingers are as stylish as any superstar's! Slip on some funky rings to draw attention to your hands, and you'll have everyone ooh-ing and ahh-ing at your gorgeous Miley manicure!

THE GLAMOUR OF HANNAH MONTANA

It's when Miley has got her Hannah wig on that all the colours come out. The Hannah Look is your chance to try some bolder shades of lip gloss and eye shadow. Maybe a rainbow across your eyelids? Or some green and purple to the corners of your eyes? Obviously you don't want to experiment on your own face, so try it on this picture of Hannah using your coloured pens.

Miley's Make-Up Tip

Before putting on make-up, your face must be smooth and soft for an even application. You should exfoliate once a week, using a warm flannel to remove dry skin and dirt. Next, massage moisturiser onto your face in a circular motion. Finally, a light-reflecting highlighter – you can use a dusting of sparkly pink or white eye shadow – patted gently onto the arch of your eyebrow and your cheekbones will give you a fresh-faced, dewy look, and is a perfect base for make-up.

GETTING THE HANNAH LOOK

Just like with the Miley Look, apply some eye shadow, blusher, eyeliner and lip gloss. What's different this time is that you really need to use lots of bright colours! Try green, different pinks, yellow and purple on your eyelids and some really red lipstick so you have that superstar pout! To finish, dip your make-up brush into some shimmer dust and carefully and lightly brush your cheeks and temples. If you want, add some sparkle to your hair and clothes. With Hannah, there is no such thing as too much.

Miley's Top Tip

To get luscious wavy locks like Miley, wash your hair before bed and after a quick blast with the blow-dryer, twist damp hair into two plaits. Undo the plaits in the morning and backcomb sections of the underside of your hair for volume. Texture and hold is achieved with a salt spray, which you can even make at home …Get yourself a spray-bottle and fill it with warm water and salt. Shake and squirt the mixture all over whilst scrunching your hair from the roots to the tips.

25

Miley and her Music

Even though her film career is bigger than ever with the release of Hannah Montana: The Movie, Miley's main goal is in becoming world-famous for her music. In her short career as a musician, Miley has performed Disney songs, Hannah Montana songs, and even gone on a Hannah tour! Now that her first solo album is out and going strong it seems that like everything else in Miley's career, it's only going up!

DISNEY! DISNEY! DISNEY!

Seeing as Disney has a long history of making some of the best songs ever, it was easy to realise that these could be made way better by adding Miley's voice to them! So in 2006 Miley made her first Disney cover, singing "Zip-a-Dee-Doo-Dah" for the *Disneymania* album, and with Miley's help this album sold almost a million copies! Miley has also made a cover of "Part of Your World" from *The Little Mermaid* and has performed several Christmas songs for Disney, such as "Rockin' around the Christmas Tree" and "Santa Claus is coming to Town", so you don't have to be without her over the holiday season!

"Song writing is what I really want to do with my life forever."

HITTING THE ROCKIN'

When the first *Hannah Montana* soundtrack came out, it stunned the music world! Not only was this the very first *Hannah Montana* album, but it came out at the same time as albums from bands who had been around way longer such as My Chemical Romance and still managed to beat them. It was number one in the charts for two weeks! Showing just how strong the *Hannah Montana* fan army was about to become…

In 2007, *Hannah Montana 2: Meet Miley Cyrus* was released. Not only was this a second *Hannah Montana* soundtrack, but it also showed us the first songs that Miley actually wrote herself. Obviously, this was an immediate number one as crowds of kids rushed out to buy it, looking forward to listening to some of Miley's own world for themselves.

"*Meet Miley Cyrus* was just meeting me, finding out who I am."

27

Miley's Interests and Hobbies

THE MILEY AND MANDY SHOW

Is there no stopping Miss Miley? Even in her free time she is making amazing shows! Miley and her BFF, Mandy Jiroux, have started creating videos for what they call The Miley and Mandy Show.

The show has everything, from the two practising hilarious dance moves or just hanging out at Miley's house. The girls are the writers, producers, directors, and also say they are responsible for hair, make-up, wardrobe and lighting – it's quite literally all their own stuff! The show has shown millions around the world how much fun you can have with your best friends when you really value them.

When the first episode went up, it took less than a month for a million people to watch it! And you can watch it too if you type this in on your computer:

YouTube - mileymandy's Channel

http://www.youtube.com/mileymandy

"For me and Mandy laughter is like sunshine to a flower, it helps it grow and be brighter and even more beautiful than it was ever expected to be. Ok, I've had my cheesy moment!"

Miley's Pet Family

In *Bolt*, Miley played a girl who cares for and loves her pet dog. This must have been really easy for Miley to do as back home she also has a dog, several in fact! Miley has become famous for having an enormous collection of animals, caring for and loving every one.

Two of Miley's dogs, Roadie and Loco, have become particularly famous for winning "most eligible pets" in a famous pet owners magazine, which lists the favourite and most famous pets of celebrity owners. If you have pets, and love them in the same way that Miley does, then you'll probably find your pets incredibly cute as well. Here is what makes Miley's two award-winning pets so adorable:

Roadie (Yorkshire Terrier)

Yorkshire Terriers are small dogs with long silky coats that run along the back and tail. These dogs are famous for being very intelligent, and though they are small, they are courageous and self-confident. Miley can frequently be seen riding her bike with Roadie, as the perky young pooch sits in her basket while she rides around Hollywood looking for some much-deserved retail therapy!

Miley's Pet Collection:
7 Horses
6 Dogs
2 Cats
A Bird
A Chicken
A Turtle

Loco (Shih Tzu)

Shih Tzus are very ancient dogs that come from
China. Just like the Yorkshire Terrier, a Shih Tzu is
very small, with plenty of fur all over its body. With it's
flat nose, it's often a very messy eater and Loco has to have
his face cleaned every time he eats! Along with the Yorkshire
Terrier, Shih Tzus are very self-confident. Because Loco
is so small, you can often find him hitching a ride with
Miley . . . in her handbag! Because Shih Tzus have so muc hair,
Miley and other owners often like to decorate it by attaching a
small bow to make the hair stand up.

Add some colour to
MiLEY'S BFFs

Here are some of Miley's favourite animals, but they're all lacking that extra spark that only a splash of colour can give them...

Miley's faithful canine ...

Why not design a glittery bow?

Miley's Ranch

On Miley's ranch, back in her hometown of Tennessee she owns several horses. Having been riding since she was two, it's safe to say that Miley is a pretty good rider! She even shows off some of her skills in *Hannah Montana: The Movie*. But it isn't just about how well the horse rides for Miley, her horses also have to be some of the most stunningly beautiful animals around! Colour in the horse above and see if you can make a stallion gorgeous enough for Miss Cyrus!

35

Use your favourite colours to create your very own saddle! ✴ ✴

MILEY'S HORSES

When she's on her ranch in Tennessee, Miley likes nothing better than to be riding round the countryside with the wind in her face. Of course she only likes the prettiest of ponies, so colour in the gorgeous horse above so it is fit for a pop princess!

Customise your own cowgirl hat here. Use as many sparkles as you like!

Make your own
GROOVY BANGLES

One of Miley's favourite accessories are her amazing collection of bangles. Try making your own by following these steps:

You will need

Two pieces of loo-roll or kitchen-towel tube

Some scissors

Paint and glitter

Ribbons, or if you can't find any then use elastic bands or string

Instructions:

1 With the loo roll or kitchen towel, strip it down so all that is left is the cardboard roll.

2 Cut the roll so that it is split in half through the middle

3 With your parents' help, pierce a small hole in all four corners of each half of the roll.

4 Use ribbon to tie each corner of the card with its equivalent corner on the other piece. It's a good idea to do this with both pieces on your wrists already, so it isn't too loose or too tight.

5 Decorate your bangles with paint, glitter or felt-tip, whichever you think will make it look the most fabulous!

If you've got it done right it should be looking wonderful as it sits snugly on your wrist, all ready for the next party!

Miley WORDSEARCH

Search for the words listed below in the grid. The words can run horizontally, diagonally or from top to bottom.

```
A  H  D  V  A  O  R  B  E  B
O  O  W  A  O  L  H  R  W  N
L  L  W  E  I  V  A  E  S  K
E  L  L  I  V  A  A  A  N  N
L  Y  L  I  N  E  L  D  K  W  S
K  W  A  N  A  T  N  O  M  M
R  O  E  H  L  A  D  U  G  I
A  O  J  O  N  E  A  T  K  L
P  D  B  O  O  S  J  A  K  E
S  S  O  H  Y  M  A  N  D  Y
```

Hidden words:

- BOLT
- BREAKOUT
- HDOG
- HOEDOWN
- HOLLYWOOD
- JAKE
- MANDY
- MONTANA
- NASHVILLE
- SEAVIEW
- SMILEY
- SPARKLE

39

Lucas Till/Travis Brody

Lucas is famous to all of us for playing Miley's crush Travis in *Hannah Montana: The Movie*. Lucas hails from Texas, but he moved to Los Angeles when he was 13, trying to balance his life at high school with his movie career. Only three weeks after graduating high school he received the role of a lifetime, finding out that he would star in the movie of *Hannah Montana*!

Filming was tough for Lucas, as not only did he have the daunting task of working alongside worldwide stars, he also had a problem when it came to his riding scenes with Miley as he didn't know how to ride! Luckily he learned quickly and now loves it so much he does it at every opportunity.

Justin Gaston

This lucky man is Miley's current boyfriend. She met the super-hunk Justin Gaston on the set of the show *Nashville Star*, which her dad Billy Ray was working on. Just like when she was going out with Nick Jonas, at first Miley was careful not to admit or deny anything, but she has recently admitted they have been dating for two years now and, thankfully, are still going strong.

Like with Nick, Miley is fortunate to have found a guy she shares the same interests and values with, allowing them to understand each other and have a stronger and longer-lasting relationship!

"He's a really great guy. He's gone through stuff, and I've gone through stuff, and everyone goes through that. I think it's really awesome that we have that in common – that we can talk about it and that we can understand each other ... he gets it."

Justin's day job is as a male model, and he has worked for some of the most famous clothing companies in the world. It was when he moved to Los Angeles that he was lucky enough to catch the eye of Miley Cyrus. When he is not working he spends a lot of time with Miley on the set of *Hannah Montana*, and they have often been seen together out and about, grabbing lunch or just a quick milkshake.

With cameras always following her, it's hard not just for Miley, but also for whoever she is dating who might not be used to being under the spotlight so often. But with Justin, who is musical, religious, but most importantly, very cute, Miley may have found someone who can be with her as she continues to wow all of us on stage and on our televisions!

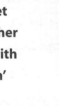

ARE MILEY AND JUSTIN COMPATIBLE?

Miley - Sagittarius

A Sagittarius is known for one thing, and that's being their own person. They seek complete freedom, but love to hang out with their friends and have a good time. They're able to grab the attention of large groups of people and entertain them.

Justin - Virgo

A Virgo is really good at noticing problems and then solving them, which always helps when they're in a relationship. A Virgo is also very dependable in times of hardship.

With Miley already a massive star, that means being her own person all the time and having to keep the thousands of adoring fans at her concerts. She is clearly very lucky to have a Virgo like Justin (and a gorgeous Virgo at that!) to rely on if things ever get stressful, and to be patient with her if she can't spend all her time with him because she's busy rockin' out for you guys!

THE LOVE SUM

If you have ever thought the maths you learn at school is useless, think again! Here is a cool sum to work out whether you and your crush are destined for true love. Here is how to do it, using Miley and Justin's names!

1 Write down your full name and the name of the person you want to test:

M-I-L-E-Y C-Y-R-U-S

J-U-S-T-I-N G-A-S-T-O-N

2 You have to count how many times each letter from the word "loves" appears in the two names:

M-I-L-E-Y C-Y-R-U-S

J-U-S-T-I-N G-A-S-T-O-N

Number of Ls -	1
Number of Os -	1
Number of Vs -	0
Number of Es -	1
Number of Ss -	3

Result: 11013

3 Now this is when the maths kicks in! You need to add each number to the number next to it, keep doing this until it reaches just two numbers:

11013,

1+1=2 1+0=1 0+1=1 1+3=4

= 2114

2+1=3 1+1=2 1+4=5

325

3+2=5 2+5=7

57

Final answer: 57%

And there you go! According to this Miley, and Justin have a 57% chance of going all the way! But remember, this is all up to you. Do you value a piece of maths or the star signs to guide you along the right path? Or does it matter more to you what you have in common, or if he makes you laugh, or if he's too cute not to be with! As Miley would tell you, it needs to feel right and most importantly, you should just follow your heart!

Things you need to know about Miley

Think you're a Miley fan? If you weren't at first you will be when you know these facts about the teen sensation...

1 Miley's goals in life are to read the entire Bible, open a school for children with disabilities, pay her Grandma's bills, visit sick children in hospitals in each of the 50 States, and to produce her little sister's first record.

2 Her Sweet 16th was held in Disneyworld, California. The park was closed down for the weekend, and each guest paid $250 to attend, with all the money going to charity.

3 For her concert tour, Miley earned a whopping million dollars a week!

4 Even though her 3-D *Best of Both Worlds* concert didn't open at every cinema in America, it still managed to beat all other films out in the whole of the country and was no.1 at the box office!

5 Miley's grandmother is the only person who still calls her Destiny.

6 One of Miley's biggest role-models is former *Lizzie Maguire* star Hilary Duff for always staying true to herself.

7 Miley may be a vegetarian, but she doesn't eat anything green.

8 She wrote her song "I Miss You" after the death of her grandfather.

9 Even though she earns millions and millions every year she doesn't get to see any of it, as her dad only gives her $300 dollars a month allowance!

10 In the Disney Channel Games she was on the green team two years in a row.

11 She broke up with her boyfriend in first grade because he wouldn't let her win in the school talent show, wanting to win it himself instead.

12 The furthest she has ever been from home is Paris, France.

13 Miley keeps a diary, and in spite of her busy schedule she tries to write in it every day!

14 One of her favourite things to do is to watch chick flicks with her sister on a rainy afternoon.

15 One of the things she hates the most is being tickled.

16 One of her favourite things to do with her horses is not riding them, it's braiding their tails!

17 She first realised she wanted to try acting when she was younger and visited the set of *Docs*, a TV show her dad was filming.

18 Even though she isn't even close to turning 18, Miley has still written over 100 songs, with some of them being used in *Hannah Montana*!

19 Emily Osment, who plays Lilly in *Hannah Montana* and is Miley's BFF in real life, is a talented knitter and taught Miley how to knit when they were on the set.

20 Most of the time she wears a ring with Love inscribed on it. The ring was a gift her father gave to her mother.

Miley at the MOVIES

HANNAH MONTANA: THE MOVIE

Ok, admit it, this is what we've all been waiting for, to have a full-length *Hannah Montana* movie that will make all other films look like a home movie by Jackson!

The film is about Miley letting the fame get to her head and becoming obsessed with being Hannah Montana, whilst living the glamorous life that being Hannah involves. Eventually she goes too far by getting into a fight with celebrity TV star Tyra Banks and then forgetting to say goodbye to Jackson because she was shopping, and missing her friend Lilly's birthday.

Knowing that this is not the real Miley we all love, her dad, Robby, decides to trick her into going with him to Tennessee by making her think that they're going to New York. While spending time in her

hometown, Crowley Corners, to think about what really matters to her in life, she also considers whether she can keep her life as Hannah Montana and stay as two people at once.

Miley spends time with her friends Lilly and Ollie, but finds it difficult to live on a ranch at first. She gets a crush on an old childhood friend. Trouble soon arises, however, when a sneaky reporter called Oswald comes to know her secret, and decides he wants to tell the whole world about Miley Stewart and Hannah Montana. Miley then realises how much she loves living in Tennessee, and starts to wonder whether she wants to choose between two lives.

One thing that does make this movie extra-special is the amazing new songs; the soundtrack to it doesn't just have amazing tracks from Hannah and Miley, but also some from her dad, Billy Ray Cyrus. The music and dance number that got everyone standing up and giving it a go in the movie, was the "Hoedown Throwdown". Kids around the world have had their eyes glued to their screens, eagerly watching Miley's videos on the internet teaching them how to pull off the song's crazy dance moves.

> "Everyone was like 'You know, we need you to write this song. And oh by the way, it's going to be you and John Travolta.' So I'm like 'Great! That's easy. Just write a song for John Travolta.'"

BOLT

Miley also hit the big screen with the film *Bolt*, though this was a little different from other things she'd starred in as it was a computer-animated film! She got to star alongside the massive movie star John Travolta, who some of you might remember as Edna Turnblad when he starred in *Hairspray* (a film I remember for having the amazingly gorgeous Zac Efron).

In the film Miley plays Penny. Penny is the star of a hit TV show (sound familiar?), which she stars in alongside a pet dog who actually believes that he is the character he is playing. When Bolt goes missing, Penny becomes very upset and it is up to Bolt to get himself back to Hollywood as he thinks someone is trying to kidnap Penny.

What made this film extra-exciting for Miley was that she got to write and sing a duet with John Travolta, who has starred in some of the most famous musical

films ever! The excitement was all too much for Miley, as it was also the first film she has starred in that has been nominated for an Oscar, the most famous film awards in the world! I wonder how long it will be until we see Miley clutching one at the awards show …

"Everything has to have a message. I just feel like there are so many movies out there that you don't take away anything from, and I really want you to take home a good feeling."

What's the news on the latest movie?
How is the boy situation?
Your last film and CD earned you over $100 million, what do you plan to spend it on?
Are you doing another album anytime soon?

THE RED CARPET

Ok, you have your outfit all designed, now it's time to cut it out and stick it on to the red carpet. You're looking gorgeous and it's now time to meet the eager paparazzi!

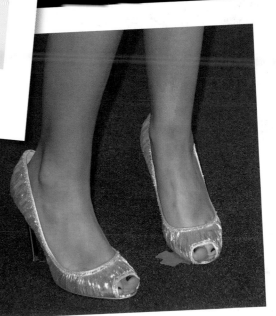

Design
YOUR OWN T-SHIRT

Is there a fashion designer in you? With the *Hannah Montana* clothing line on the shelves, have you ever thought about designing some clothes yourself? Try sketching designs for a t-shirt so cool even Miss Miley herself would wear it.

How to give it some added coolness:

Try putting glitter on it to give it that extra sparkle.

Think about the colours, do you want it one colour and then add lots of detail? Or do you want it to be jazzy and multi-coloured?

A cool slogan draws attention to a lot of t-shirts, it could be something about Miley and Hannah or just one of your favourite catchphrases.

How do you want the t-shirt shaped, short-sleeved or long-sleeved? Baggy or figure-hugging? Plenty of accessories attached or nice and simple? These all affect how your t-shirt will turn out.

Now comes the time to draw that design you have in your head on to the t-shirt. Remember that it's important to already have a plan of what you want in your design before you start drawing.

MILEY

HANNAH

MILEY

HANNAH

(miley)

Are you happy with it? Would you wear it yourself?
If you want to make your design a reality you could
give it a go by buying a plain white t-shirt and using
paints and glitter to bring your ideas to life!

So it's been another year at the top for Miss Miley Cyrus and no doubt she'll be singing and dancing all the way through 2011. Watch this space to find out!

ANSWERS

p20 Crossword

1. Justin Gaston
2. Eleven
3. Mandy Jiroux
4. Seven Things
5. Breakout
6. Smiley

7. Zoe Stewart
8. Roadie
9. Cheat it
10. Destiny
11. Zip-a-Dee-Doo-Dah
12. Braison

p39 Miley Wordsearch

```
A H D V A O R B E B
O O W A O L H R W N
I L W E I V A E S K
E L L I V H S A N N
L Y I N E L D K W S
K W A N A T N O M M
R O E H L A D U G I
A O J O N E A T K L
P D B O O S J A K E
S S O H Y M A N D Y
```

PICTURE CREDITS

Getty: 2, 4 (bottom), 5 (top), 6, 7, 10, 11, 12, 16 (top right), 20, 21, 22 (left), 23, 24 (top left), 26, 27, 28 (bottom left, top right), 29, 30, 31, 32 (left centre), 37 (top right), 38, 39, 40, 41, 42, 43, 44, 45, 46, 47, 48, 49, 50, 51, 53, 55 (assorted), 57, 58, 59, 60, 63

Rex: 8 (top left), 9, 13, 14, 15, 16 (bottom left), 17, 18, 19, 25, 32 (top right), 33 (top left, right and centre)

PA Photos: 4 (top), 8 (bottom left), 52   Corbis: 5 (bottom), 28 (right centre)

iStockphoto: 22 (bottom right), 24 (top right), 33 (bottom right), 37 (bottom right), 55 (assorted)

ACKNOWLEDGEMENTS

Posy Edwards would like to thank Tim Edwards, Amanda Harris, Naomi Bacon, Helen Ewing, James Martindale, Jane Sturrock, Briony Hartley and Rich Carr.

Copyright © Posy Edwards 2009

The right of Posy Edwards to be identified as the author of this work has been asserted in accordance with the Copyright, Designs and Patents Act 1988.

First published in hardback in Great Britain in 2009 by

Orion Books an imprint of the Orion Publishing Group Ltd Orion House, 5 Upper St Martin's Lane, London WC2H 9EA An Hachette Livre UK Company

1 3 5 7 9 10 8 6 4 2

All rights reserved. Apart from any use permitted under UK copyright law, this publication may only be reproduced, stored or transmitted, in any form, or by any means, with prior permission in writing of the publishers or, in the case of reprographic production, in accordance with the terms of licences issued by the Copyright Licensing Agency.

A CIP catalogue record for this book is available from the British Library.

ISBN: 978 1 4091 1332 4

Designed by Goldust Design Printed in Italy by Rotolito

The Orion Publishing Group's policy is to use papers that are natural, renewable and recyclable and made from wood grown in sustainable forests. The logging and manufacturing processes are expected to conform to the environmental regulations of the country of origin.

Every effort has been made to fulfil requirements with regard to reproducing copyright material. The author and publisher will be glad to rectify any omissions at the earliest opportunity.

www.orionbooks.co.uk